BEHIND THE SCENES BIOGRAPHIES

WHAT YOU NEVER KNEW ABOUT

>>> ———————————— <<<

SELENA
GOMEZ

by Dolores Andral

CAPSTONE PRESS
a capstone imprint

Spark is published by Capstone Press, an imprint of Capstone
1710 Roe Crest Drive, North Mankato, Minnesota 56003
capstonepub.com

Library of Congress Cataloging-in-Publication Data
Names: Andral, Dolores, author.
Title: What you never knew about Selena Gomez / by Dolores Andral.
Description: North Mankato, Minnesota : Spark, an imprint of Capstone Press, [2023] | Series: Behind the scenes biographies | Includes bibliographical references and index. | Audience: Ages 9–11. | Audience: Grades 4–6. | Summary: "Do you know what career Selena Gomez would choose if she wasn't a singer and actor? Find out this and more when you crack open this book. High-interest details and bold photos of her fascinating life will enthrall readers"—Provided by publisher.
Identifiers: LCCN 2022024626 (print) | LCCN 2022024627 (ebook) | ISBN 9781669003151 (hardcover) | ISBN 9781669040613 (paperback) | ISBN 9781669003113 (pdf) | ISBN 9781669003137 (kindle edition)
Subjects: LCSH: Gomez, Selena, 1992– Juvenile literature. | Actresses—United States—Biography—Juvenile literature. | Singers—United States—Biography—Juvenile literature. | LCGFT: Biographies.
Classification: LCC PN2287.G585 A53 2023 (print) | LCC PN2287.G585 (ebook) | DDC 791.4302/8/092 [B]—dc23/eng/20220711
LC record available at https://lccn.loc.gov/2022024626
LC ebook record available at https://lccn.loc.gov/2022024627

Editorial Credits
Editor: Erika L. Shores; Designer: Heidi Thompson; Media Researcher: Jo Miller; Production Specialist: Tori Abraham

TABLE OF CONTENTS

Words in **bold** are in the glossary.

NOMBRE
MEANS NAME

Could you imagine Selena Gomez by any other nombre? She was almost called Priscilla. But one of her cousins was named that first. Instead, Selena was named after Selena Quintanilla. She was known as the queen of **Tejano** music.

Selena Quintanilla

SHOW US WHAT YOU KNOW,
SELENATORS!

1. How many of Selena's rescue dogs can you name?

2. What was the name of Selena's first band?

3. Where's a weird place Selena has met a fan?

4. How many Spanish language albums has Selena made?

5. What does Selena sometimes say when she's shocked?

Selena Gomez & The Scene

1. Daisy, Winnie, Baylor, Wallace, Fina, Chip, Willie, Chazz

2. Selena Gomez & The Scene **3.** A bathroom

4. One Spanish album **5.** "Oh, My Lanta!"

SELENA'S
SKILLS

People know Selena as a great singer. But she's also an actor. She's the voice of Mavis in the *Hotel Transylvania* movies. Selena hasn't always liked her voice. She said she thought it was too low.

FACT

Selena stars with Martin Short and Steve Martin in the TV series *Only Murders in the Building.*

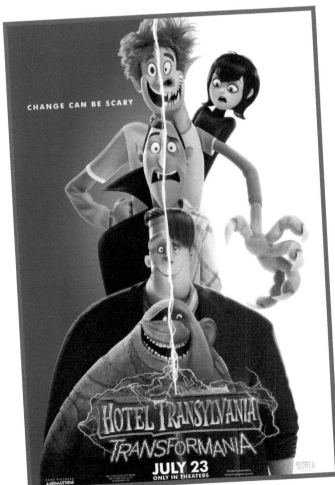

What would Selena be if she wasn't a singer and actor? Maybe a chef! She hosts a TV series called *Selena + Chef*. Selena learns how to make food from all over the world.

SELENA'S MUSIC

Selena has made seven albums. She has sold more than 6 million albums. Her songs have reached 40 million in downloads and ringtones. Her songs and videos have been **streamed** billions of times.

FACT

Selena drinks olive oil to protect her singing voice.

In 2021, Selena's album *Revelación* came out. It's her first album in Spanish. She says it's easier for her to sing in Spanish than it is to speak it.

Revelación was up for Best Latin Pop Album at the **Grammys**. It's the first time Selena's music has had this honor.

"It's always a bit nerve-racking before releasing any music because as artists we put so much of ourselves out there."

—Selena Gomez (*Billboard*, March 2021)

Selena made two music videos using iPhones. One video, "Lose You to Love Me," used one iPhone. Another video, "Look at Her Now," used about 20 iPhones. Selena's grandparents were on the video set with her. They took home iPhones as gifts!

WOULD YOU TRY IT?

Sometimes Selena eats Oreos with a fork. Why? She says it's easier to dunk them into milk. She also likes to dip her popcorn in pickle juice. Her other favorite snack? Fritos covered in melted cheese, chili, and onions. Yum!

BIG SISTER
SELENA

At age 20, Selena became a big sister. She loves it. She thinks of herself as a role model. She has two sisters. She took one of them to the *Frozen II* **premiere**. They both dressed up as ice princesses. Brr!

BEST FRIENDS
FOR LIFE

Selena and Francia

Selena has lots of best friends. One of them saved her life! Selena has a disease called **lupus**. It damaged her kidneys. Her BFF Francia Raisa gave Selena one of hers.

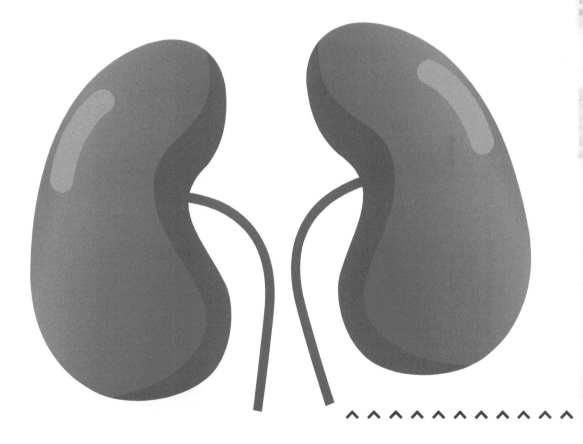

Another one of Selena's best friends calls her Rosebud. Cara Delevingne and Selena got matching rosebud tattoos. Selena has at least 15 tattoos. Many of them have special meanings.

Selena and Cara

Selena has the word *sunshine* tattooed on her right foot.

FACT

Selena was the first person to reach 100 million followers on Instagram.

SPEAKING UP!

Selena uses her music to speak her mind. She helps other people speak up by telling their stories. She helped create the TV series *Living Undocumented*.

Selena's show follows families as they try to become U.S. **citizens**. Two of Selena's grandparents came from Mexico. It took them many years to become citizens.

Selena has a beauty brand called Rare Beauty. She wants people to feel good about how they look. She also wants to bring attention to **mental health**. She hopes to raise $100 million through her brand. One percent of sales goes to supporting mental health services.

"*Figuring out how to manage my own mental health hasn't always been easy, but it's something I am constantly working on. I hope I can help others work on it too.*"

—Selena Gomez (Change.org, 2021)

Glossary

citizen (SI-tuh-zuhn)—a person who is a member of a country either because of being born there or being declared a member by law

Grammys (GRAM-ees)—an awards show for the music industry

lupus (LOO-pus)—a disease in which the body's immune system attacks itself; it can lead to skin, lung, and liver problems

mental health (MEN-tuhl HELTH)—the condition of one's mind and emotions

premiere (pruh-MIHR)—the first public viewing of a movie or play

rescue dogs (RES-kyoo DAWGS)—dogs that had been homeless

stream (STREEM)—to send or receive data such as music and video over the internet

Tejano (TAY-anoh)—a style of Mexican American music that blends American music with traditional Mexican music

Read More

Menéndez, Juliet. *Latinitas: Celebrating 40 Big Dreamers.* New York: Godwin Books; Henry Holt and Company, 2021.

Reynolds, Luke. *Braver than I Thought: Real People. Real Courage. Real Hope.* New York: Aladdin, 2022.

Internet Sites

18 Interesting Facts About Selena Gomez
ohfact.com/interesting-facts-about-selena-gomez/

50 Fun Facts About Selena Gomez
thefactsite.com/selena-gomez-facts/

Selena Gomez Official Site
selenagomez.com/

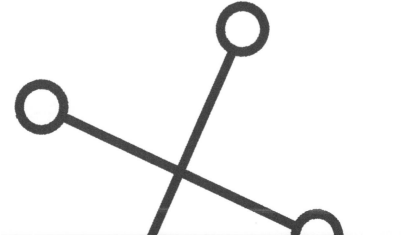

Index

About the Author

Dolores Andral earned an MFA from Queens University in Charlotte, NC. She loves writing for kids because she believes children should see themselves reflected in the books they read. She lives with her husband and four kids in Washington State.